ABANDONED
NORTHERN
IOWA

JULIE BRONSON

AMERICA
THROUGH TIME®
ADDING COLOR TO AMERICAN HISTORY

America Through Time is an imprint of Fonthill Media LLC
www.through-time.com
office@through-time.com

Published by Arcadia Publishing by arrangement with Fonthill Media LLC
For all general information, please contact Arcadia Publishing:
Telephone: 843-853-2070
Fax: 843-853-0044
E-mail: sales@arcadiapublishing.com
For customer service and orders:
Toll-Free 1-888-313-2665

www.arcadiapublishing.com

First published 2019

Copyright © Julie Bronson 2019

ISBN 978-1-63499-182-7

Typeset in Trade Gothic 10pt on 15pt
Printed and bound in England

CONTENTS

Here is a huge barn, silo, and other attachments waiting for time and nature to swallow it up.

ACKNOWLEDGMENTS

I would first like to thank my incredibly patient husband, Doug, for putting up with my absence while traveling the countryside to get as many shots of these houses and barns as I could while they are still here. He also tolerates the endless hours I spend loading and editing photos and picking out the best ones to share. Next, thank you to my friend, LeAnn, who has never said no to a day of picture taking and also helps me edit. Thank you also to my friend, Susie Crane, who makes my mixed-up sentences make sense.

One of the few houses left in Otranto.

INTRODUCTION

I never would have thought the houses and barns I love to photograph so much would be as appealing to others as they are to me. When I began this new hobby, I had no one to share my photos with. I just kept them tucked away. Then, I discovered there were more people than I could have ever imagined that were interested in them. I started to print my photos and share them online and sell the prints in stores. Now I have enough collected that I can put together a few books to share with many more people.

Boarded-up school in Otranto.

Tenold Creamery in fall colors.

This is the house at Tenold. What was once a huge beautiful old house now lays in a heap of jumbled timber.

ABANDONED NORTHERN IOWA

I owa is a land of corn and soybean fields as far as the eye can see. Cleverly hidden among the green fields of summer and the brown or white fields of winter are glimpses from the past. Beautifully weathered houses and barns are left to fend for themselves. They peek out from clusters of trees at the far end of a long driveway. happear to have had traffic off and on over the years. Farmers will use the driveway to access fields or a storage shed on the farm site. Often, you can't even see any buildings until you are into the farmyard. Many of the buildings are trapped in vegetation.

Here is what is left of what may have been a chicken house.

This cute little house was in Northwood until it was taken down a few years ago.

The adorable trim on this house was covered by the red vines.

This was a drive-by. We couldn't see a driveway, only a field.

One of many houses left to slowly be reclaimed by nature.

Above: Fence frames are fun, too.

Left: I used an old fencepost to frame the shot of a beautiful old house.

Above: Lonely old barn out in the middle of a field.

Right: Tree is the hugger.

A skeleton roof is making way for all sorts of weather to enter.

A giant pink barn. Red barns painted white will turn pink over time.

As I travel the backroads of northern Iowa, I look for those clues to help me find an old abandoned farm place just waiting for me and my camera to wander up and take photos. I take these pictures to document the way people used to build and place the buildings back when the focus was on the farm. This was long before people had outside jobs and could go to the store to buy whatever they wanted at the drop of a hat. People used to have a structure built for every need: a house, barn, chicken house, pig house, horse stable, and, of course, a silo. Don't forget the all-important outhouse! Barns ranged from small to huge old beasts.

I was told that the acreage this was on with house and other out-buildings was going to get buried, so I got a few shots of the house. When I noticed this little shed leaning to the north, I gave it a few minutes of my time.

Left: This silo appears to be missing some of the galvanized tin that was curved into a tunnel on the side of the silo to throw the silage down, but the rest is mostly intact.

Below: Chicken coop still has the roost.

Cold outhouse.

The Clubhouse. Imagine a few young kids staking claim to this little corner of the world.

I wonder if these buildings all sitting in a line were originally placed there or if they have been moved after they were done being used to clear a path to push snow. There is a nice variety of outbuildings here, including a summer kitchen on the far right.

Lots of tires end up abandoned near these old sheds.

Above: A well pump out near the barn. The barn and pump are long gone now.

Right: A skinny barn that appeared to be holding up really well, but it was destroyed along with the rest of the acreage. You can no longer tell there was ever a home where it used to sit.

This seemed to be a pretty sturdy outhouse, except for the roof.

The cute little barn lost its battle with time and Mother Nature in the winter of 2019. I am glad I took many photos of it over the years.

Right: The tiger lilies surrounding this little outhouse had me hooked!

Below: I was told by a friend about a silo inside a barn west of Lake Mills and given the owner's name. I called him and met him there to take photos. There is no trace of the silo from the outside so I was pleasantly surprised to see this on the inside. The wood is in such great condition, even though the roof is beginning to have issues.

My Iowa journey into the abandoned began with an old corn crib. It was on a main road to my friend's house. I could see it from the curve in the road about a mile away, sitting at the back of the woods. There was a narrow driveway leading to it and, one frosty morning, I just could not resist stopping to take a few pictures of it. I have always loved taking pictures of old stuff, but didn't think anyone else would give a hoot about it. I posted them online at a photo sharing site someone told me about. They were very well received, so I got to thinking maybe I wasn't the only one who enjoyed this kind of thing. I decided to go out to find more. And boy did I find a bunch! I would go out scouting one day and later my friend and I would go together to check out what I found. I don't like going alone for safety reasons. Once I started really looking for these abandoned places and recognizing the clues that lead me to them, they really started to jump out at me. If I found a place that had neighbors nearby, I would stop in to ask them if they were the owner, or if they knew the owner, and if it would be ok to take some photos. Some people just didn't understand the fascination. They had been farming around or near the place for decades and all they could see was a big ugly house that needed to be burned. They just hadn't had the time to do it yet. Others would gladly let me go take photos. "Just don't go inside," they would often say. I promised not to. Most of the places are so bad that I wouldn't want to go inside anyway. The floors are rotten, which is why so many of my shots are taken from a window or doorway. Getting to go into a house and wander around is fun though, if it's safe. If not, details like colors of paint and light fixtures are easy to see from most windows and doors, so entry isn't necessary to get photos shots.

Frosty corn crib near Northwood.

This house was all there when I first started taking photos of it. It gradually got worse and is now completely down.

Left: If you look close you can see the chimney in the stairwell. I wonder how many heads ran in to it.

Below: It seems like the porch is usually one of the first things to go.

I love old light fixtures. This is one of my favorites. It was in a house near the casino. The house was taken down quite a while ago. I doubt anyone would have saved this beautiful piece of history though.

Here are a couple of cool things you don't see every day. One is a well pump and I would almost bet it still works! The other is a double corn crib.

Above left: Standing in the barn using the doorway to frame the shot.

Above right: Looking through the upstairs window you can clearly see the chimney that for some reason has survived even though the roof is gone.

Below: Another house just hiding out in the trees.

Pink, green, yellow, and blue were very popular colors. Wallpapers came in many patterns and are still visible in some places where time hasn't peeled them away. One house that was abandoned and soon to be torn down had a "birthing" room. The owner said the midwife would come here to help with the birth of many children. It was a lovely shade of pink, as you can see. This place also had an awesome outhouse in the back that was sitting all wonky. I took pictures of it as well. It was such a shame they decided to take this lovely house down. If I could have moved it to my place, I would have.

The birthing room in a house near Manly shortly before they tore down the beautiful little home.

Pretty in pink.

So many times I see things like this I want to rush in to save, but stealing is not something I am willing to do. My hope is that the owners will come to realize the value of the relics they have before they push these places over with bulldozers.

Above left: I love the wallpaper and I wish I could save those pantry doors!

Above right: I try to find the stairwells in as many houses as I can to get pictures of them. They have so many stories to tell.

On rare occasions, when I step through to a clearing at the end of a long driveway, it feels like time came to a stop there many years ago. Far from any road traffic or neighbor noises, I feel the complete silence. It appears that this is one place the vandals missed. The doors on the house were tightly closed and locked, and the windows were unbroken and not boarded up. As much as I would love to be able to enter the house to see what the inside looks like, I was content with my outdoor shots, knowing the inside was safe and secure and untouched by destructive people. The only damage I saw had been done by trees that had fallen into sheds or across a roof or sidewalk. Respectfully, I walked around each building trying to capture little details others may overlook. I like to pick out the small things like a fancy piece of trim to finish out a corner few people would ever see. I take my photos then leave as quietly as I came. I would never disturb the silence or the beauty of a place that time seems to have forgotten. I feel comfortable wandering about a place such as this and don't worry about any unexpected surprises waiting around a corner for me, which I will mention later. I made my way back out of the yard and turned one last time to say goodbye.

This is Irv's house. I only know that because of the mailbox laying in the ditch with his name on it. The roof on this house is keeping it from rotting too fast, but the door that should be closed is almost always open when I visit, letting in the critters and weather. If I keep closing the door, maybe it will outlive me.

This house near Manly sits close to a new house. I am not sure if the dish was there for the new house or if the people who lived in this house used it before moving out, but it sure looks out of place.

I think they kept paint on this house just to make it look lived in. But the holes near the roof made by the four-legged animals that moved in gave away its emptiness.

This is the outer shot of the house with the pink birthing room. How anyone could tear this down is a mystery to me. It is more beautiful (in my opinion) than anything being built today.

Not all windows are broken by vandals.

I like to think about the people who built these buildings so long ago. Was it the farmer himself who put up all the structures? Or was it a traveling crew that went from farm to farm putting up buildings? Did the farmer save every extra kernel of corn to sell in order to be able to buy it? Did he have to borrow money from the bank or relatives to build it? Maybe a neighbor would go in with him and they would buy it together to store grain. I can picture in my mind each board being cut and nailed up and farmers working well into the night to get as much done as possible, then waking up early the next day to work on it some more. Farming back then must have been extremely difficult but satisfying. So many chores had to be done with none of the modern conveniences we have now. Every passing year would see yet another necessary structure put up as the family grew. More cattle were needed for milk and meat as were chickens for eggs, so more buildings went up to hold them. The silo had to go up to hold silage to feed the cattle over winter. Pretty soon, the entire yard was sprinkled with strategically placed sheds to house and feed all inhabitants of the farm, people, and animals.

We set out to take photos one foggy morning thinking the whole time we should have just cancelled and stayed home. Hoping we might drive out of it, we kept going. We saw these barns appear and decided it was perfect.

Another well-worn massive barn with no life inside.

Connected silos near Lake Mills. They're gone now.

I believe this was a chicken house.

Lichen always catches my eye, especially on a neat little barn like this one.

Just below the roofline you can see that the siding was protected from the elements and has not weathered as much as the rest.

Crumbling barn near Lake Mills.

I lean sideways.

A huge garden was a must for the farmers. They would grow and can enough to get them through long, cold, Iowa winters. There were some fortunate people able to have a summer kitchen just steps away from the house. They would use this building, set away from the main house, in the summer, to do all the canning and cooking. The wood cookstove burning in the house would have made it unbearable to live in, and especially to sleep in. It was already plenty warm and there were no fans! Threshing crews would come to the farms to pick the oats and make hay, so the kitchen was used to cook huge meals for them as well. Few are left standing. You can sometimes tell its identity by the remnants of a chimney.

Summer kitchen near Manly.

Above left: Chimney in a summer kitchen.

Above right: I see quite a few old woodstoves like this when I am out and about. The house this one was in got buried, so I imagine the stove is six feet under as well.

Opposite above: A summer kitchen made of salt glazed brick.

Opposite below: A summer kitchen used for cooking, feeding big threshing crews, and canning.

When a house is sitting empty for so many years, it's almost as if they have a big target painted on them for vandals coming in and ransacking. They pull drawers out and dump them, break windows, bust doors off their hinges, paint on the walls with spray paint, flip over appliances that are left behind, and even rip the sinks right off the wall. It seems as if they will do anything to trash the place. It breaks one's heart to see a place violated that was once so lovingly decorated and furnished.

Another item I would love to have room for at home. The old icebox sits way back inside this old house. I love the arched doorway, too.

So many treasures waiting to be rediscovered. Someone must have thought them treasures to begin with for them to be stashed here. The house is now gone, along with the treasures.

The fieldstone used in this basement must have taken hours to collect. There had to have been lots of strong people involved with gathering and assembling them into a cellar or basement.

I spotted this house from a long ways away. Even after taking photos of it the first time, I thought it was brick. Turns out it is tarpaper that looks like brick. The owners had a whole mess of railroad ties piled up around it.

The pretty window trim makes one wonder about the people who built this house. Did he pick it out to surprise her or did she insist on having the prettiest trim available?

What the vandals don't ruin, the critters that get in destroy. Broken-down doors and windows provide entry to a warm living space. They crawl in the drawers and make nests and use the entire house as a "litter box," causing your eyes to start watering from the smell before you poke your head in. The rain and snow saturate everything and soon the process of decay begins. The floors stay soaked and mold grows. The mold turns black and eats away at the wood. After a few years, the boards begin to falter and the floor sinks into the basement. The upstairs soon follows. The wood around the chimney also weakens and the bricks fall away. Sometimes the weight of the chimney brings a house down from the middle.

Once the roof goes, the rest follows quickly.

How does a house just fall apart like this?

Inside the fancy house near Carpenter. The floors were collapsing.

Above: Brick-patterned tin siding on a house near Northwood. It has been taken down.

Below left: This little guy watched us very closely for a while, then curled his head under for a nap. He must have thought we were okay.

Below right: Standing in the barn looking out the window at the old farmhouse.

It makes me wonder why these places were abandoned in the first place. The conclusions I have come to are simple. Kids grow up and see how much work and how difficult farming is, so they decide to go into a different career instead. They go off to college and end up working in a totally different field. The farm grows to an unmanageable size for just the farmer and his wife to take care of since the children left. They no longer need a big garden or many animals to feed just the two of them. The farmer will rent his land out to the big farmer next door and keep just one cow, a pig and some chickens. They will grow a small garden and can a few items; but, it is so much easier to drive to town for a can of beans or a jug of milk. When Mr. Farmer passes away, Mrs. Farmer is left to care for what is left of the farm. She has some help from the neighbors for a while but soon tires of the loneliness and chores all by herself. None of the children want to live on the farm, so she sells the acreage to the big farmer who is renting the land. He rents out the house for a while until the renters decide that living way out in the country, in a big old drafty house with a long driveway, isn't much fun, especially when the heating bill comes, and the driveway needs to have the snow plowed. The renter moves out. The farmer can't find another renter, so the house gets locked up and left. He will mow around the house for a while to make it look lived in. The vandals might stay away for a while but eventually they will find it and party there. The downhill slide begins. I have been watching a few houses that appeared to be lived in because of the upkeep of the yard; but the holes in the roof that appear from a fallen branch don't get fixed or a broken window gets a board instead of a pane of glass put in. These are dead giveaways. I will shoot a few photos of them if I get a chance, but often, after the signs of abandonment begin to appear, the owner will take the house down to avoid vandals trashing it. Another reason for abandonment is the owner will end up in the hospital and then a nursing home. The owner will fully believe he is getting out and want everything to stay the same, but everyone knows he will not be coming home. When he dies, the family picks through the items they want and leave the rest. Some people care nothing about the value of heirlooms or have no sentimental attachment to material things, so they lock the doors and leave it all there.

Just sit back and imagine the stories the walls of this house could tell.

I loved the rusty fence for framing the red roof.

A closet full of memories gone forever now. Were they outgrown or did they outlive the owners?

Many old houses appear to have been added onto to make room for bigger families. The addition, in one case, was not as structurally sound as the first part of the house, so it ended up falling apart. In Iowa, I have seen a couple of limestone houses; one is just north of Mason City and another is near Carpenter. The one near Mason City is starting to crumble badly on the south and west sides, but the charm of it is still very noticeable. The house near Carpenter is the one that was added on to with a wooden structure, which is falling apart. There is another place called Fort Severson near this small house that the state, or someone, maintains, also made of limestone.

The wooden addition on this limestone house is going to be gone long before the sturdy stone of the original house.

This is one of the oldest structures near Mason City. I was told by the owners that it was built in 1865.

Often the foundations of the houses and barns are made with fieldstone. The size of some of the rocks is amazing. I wonder how they placed them where they wanted to put them. Some are squared off to make nice even walls but many are put together like a puzzle. I can barely put together a puzzle with a picture to follow and am in awe of the people who assembled these foundations. The mortar they used to hold them together must be just as durable. Walls that have been standing for decades appear to be as strong as the day they were built. It seems as if the only thing that can penetrate these stone walls is a tree that decides to grow right next to them. The roots push everything out of the way, instead growing around things. Eventually, the foundation is pushed in and collapses from the pressure. Then the wall it was holding up slowly begins to buckle from the weight.

Liability is a big concern for people with abandoned places, especially the barns. The trend nowadays is to have barnwood features in your house. People use it for picture frames, shelving, and signs. Some use entire walls for the basement or den and cover the bar with it. I think they are quite unaware that the smells that permeate the wood from the inside, from when it was on the barn, have a good chance of still being there. Once brought into an enclosed area like a basement or den, they begin to emerge. The smell of hog or cow poo is not so pleasant in one's home! So out goes the wood. Corrugated tin which has the rusty charm of an old barn may be attempted next to replace the wood. It doesn't stink quite so much.

Square cut stones for foundations are quite common. There must have been many full-time jobs for stone masons back then!

Jars and jugs lay strewn about on the floor. Fieldstone walls of the cellar/basement are much more sturdy than the wood house above.

Back to the liability. My friend, LeAnn, and I were taking pictures of a friend's barn when he came thundering in in his big pickup. He said the neighbor up the road called him and said someone was poking around his barn site. When he found out it was us, he was fine with us being there. But he did say that people had been stealing barnwood from his barn, which you can tell from the first picture I have here. He told me that he was afraid someone was going to get hurt trying to steal, so he was going to have to burn it down. He had offered it to a group of people, but they only wanted to take the useable stuff and were going to leave him a mess to clean up, so he said he would just light a match to it instead. I begged him to give me a call before he had the fire. He did! One April morning, after we had just gotten a dusting of snow, he called me. I hurried down to the location and he lit the match. There was plenty of old firewood in the barn that was as light as paper, and the haymow had quite a bit of hay, so the fire went fast. I walked in a semi-circle around it, back and forth, getting shots, and was it ever hot! It was only the two of us and one old woodchuck that left as soon as he figured out what was going on. The burning barn is one of my favorite, though saddest, shots. I would much rather see an old barn stand until it is ready to fall on its own, or better yet, have someone save it from destruction.

Left: All of the siding didn't fall off this barn by itself. People were stealing it for their "home improvement" projects.

Below: One of my favorite shots ever! You could tell the heat was overwhelming. I could only walk around the front and left side as the other two sides were too hot. I took many shots that day, but this one is the best.

When wood is worn down by weather, the tin begins to rust and lose its grip.

A big barn near Nora Springs.

Bare Bones Barn. The siding has been taken, most likely for home decorating projects.

But restoring old barns is not lucrative anymore. New pole sheds are easier to put up and roofs don't need shingles. Very few keep cattle in them any longer and they don't make very good storage sheds. Lots of wood and windows are stored in them as well as other things, but the majority of them sit empty. There is one south of me that I have been watching for quite some time. It began to fall by just squatting down on the backside. I thought as soon as I saw that, it wouldn't be long before it was totally down, but it has taken a couple of years to get to the point it is at now. It is still not all the way down, but the roof is starting to break apart because of the weird twist on the beams. A couple of my other favorite barns have been abandoned for many years as well. I have been taking pictures of them at different stages of dilapidation. I lost one this past winter that I have been taking shots of for nearly ten years. It really didn't look that bad the last time I was there, but the heavy snow we had this past winter was too much for it.

This is how this barn first looked when I noticed it squatting.

Taking its own sweet time sinking back to the earth.

Looks like peeling sunburn.

The siding is either falling off or being taken off for projects.

There was a huge owl sitting in a tree watching us as we approached this barn. I didn't get any good pictures of it before it took off; but it was as if it were protecting this place.

Gently falling back to earth.

The hopeful woman that lives in the house on this farm said she hopes to restore this barn one day. I am afraid she may have waited too long.

A window frame used for photo framing works almost every time. I love the glazed brick and the skeleton roof.

There are many houses that I have been watching for a few years. They make you think they will be in a heap the next time you visit, but they are still standing tall and proud as if they are fighting to stay upright, with basements caving in, trees laying across the roofs, and holes chewed through the siding by critters, all things that should have crumpled them into a pile of sawdust. Still, they hang on.

This house being used for storage of lumber and windows is no longer with us. It was so photogenic!

A good solid foundation doesn't mean the house will stay good and solid without some attention. This house has been taken down.

This huge house was amazing in its detail. I can't believe it was abandoned.

This was a big house in Tenold. I could be wrong, but I thought I heard the people say it used to be a hotel and post office. You can tell there used to be a heating stove on the upper level, because of the chimney that is still there. The entire place lays in a heap now. The past winter was too much for it to bear.

Horses were pastured around this house and it isn't noticeable in this picture, but they gnawed on the wood on the house until it looked very smooth and cool! It is gone now.

The bright colors in beautifully painted kitchens don't seem to fade away with time, even though the doors and windows are long gone. This old wood stove stands on a floor that should have been in the basement years ago. The curtains hung with love years ago catch every breeze that flows through. They keep waving to the passersby in hopes of attracting attention. An old jacket hangs on a hook near the door waiting for someone to come by and put it on, maybe go out to feed the barn animals. Jars of all sizes and shapes lay in heaps in the basement where the critters or vandals knocked them down.

If I had a strong back and a huge house, I would try to gather up all of the old wood stoves I see in my travels.

Right: It appears this chore jacket got hung on the nail only to never have its owner return to do more chores.

Below: I just can't get over the bright, cheerful colors used in this kitchen.

Some of these places can be a bit scary when approaching. You just don't know what you may find. The possibility of running into people doing drugs or making them is real, but luckily, I have never had that happen. I'm more likely to run into a scary critter. One time we were taking photos of a fallen house and we could hear growling of some kind. It sounded mean! We didn't hang around. We also saw a skunk hiding under a pile of wood in a silo. We quietly backed away from that potential stink bomb. At another place, we discovered a pile of poached deer. That's another place we hastily left.

This is Irv's house. It had a mailbox lying in the ditch next to the driveway with his name on it. It is one house that is still in very good shape because the roof is still solid. The problem is whenever I get to this house, I must shut the door. I only just step into the front room and it feels to me like this house is still alive. I don't want to intrude, but the dang vandals keep leaving the door open, so I shut it. It has a beautiful porch with lovely gingerbread trim in an attractive shade of blue. I imagine one of the times I visit, the vandals will have destroyed it.

Irv's house. I love everything about this house. From the red roof to the gingerbread on the porch to the blue screen door.

Trim on Irv's house.

There is one home near Silver Lake that I drove by many times and took pictures of because it was the beautiful shade of gray that I love so much. It had six-pane windows and was a two-story house. One day driving by, I caught a glimpse of logs in the walls. This house that I loved so much was a log cabin under the siding! Well, I couldn't just take photos from the road anymore. I had to go visit the owner. They live in a house on the same acreage. He let me wander around and take as many photos as I wanted and let me bring LeAnn back to take some, too. LeAnn is my photo-taking friend. She loves these old houses and barns as much as I do. It is great to have someone with the same passion to share the experience with. When we go to a new place, she will go one direction and I go the opposite. When our paths cross, we can point out things to each other to shoot so we don't miss anything. It's safer having someone else there too.

A two-story log cabin near Silver Lake.

One place we stumbled upon was a tiny little shack next to Deer Creek. It was perfect for pictures. It was up a short winding driveway. We parked on the road and walked up to it. When we peeked inside, there was a sleeping bag and a chair. Luckily, no one was home. That was kind of creepy. I admit, it looked like it had been a long time since the sleeping bag had been slept in, but who really knows. It was strange because it was miles from anything.

Above: An old log cabin in the woods near Northwood. We got scolded for being out here taking pictures, because it was hunting season and we didn't have blaze orange on. Who knew? We took our photos and got out of there before they thought we were deer!

Right: Surprise inside. This is the shed we found with a sleeping bag inside. It was a bit creepy.

There are many little towns in Iowa that only have a few people still living in them. They have a zip code and a sign outside of town, but all the businesses have closed and the schools are boarded up. The kids ride the bus for many miles to get to the consolidated schools. There might be a church left in town still having services but some of those are closed as well. There is a town called Otranto that has a closed school and a few houses left. It had a beautiful abandoned bridge that I took many shots of before they took it down. It had the neatest pilings or foundation on the riverbanks. The huge blocks that held it up were made of limestone. It had the dreaded "DO NOT ENTER" sign on it, but I was able to take many shots from close by. They finally removed it a couple of years ago, but I really don't know why they did. It was a beautiful reminder of the past. Not everyone sees these things the way I do, however.

Abandoned school in the small town of Britt.

Otranto bridge. It has been taken down. I suppose safety was a concern. Too bad. So much history gone.

Footings of the Otranto bridge. Huge blocks of limestone.

There are a few creameries left in northern Iowa that are no longer functioning as creameries. Instead, they are used as storehouses. People have so much dang stuff these days. I am guilty of it just as bad as anyone. The towns of Hanlontown and Silver Lake have small ones still standing. There used to be a town called Tenold that is all but gone. The creamery there was only just beginning to cave in when I first saw it, but now the entire roof is almost gone. Across the road from the Tenold creamery there used to be a hardware store and a huge house with a post office in it. The house is nearly gone, and the hardware store was in a crumpled heap the first time I saw it, but it has been removed. I saw some interesting things in the pile of crumbled wood, but I doubt any of it was saved. The barn on this site was nice when I first photographed it but half of it has lost the battle with time now too. There is a beautiful wooden silo with a very interesting roof that should be saved, but no one does that sort of thing anymore, I guess. I try to get down there every year to take pictures of the progress of the demise of all the buildings. Every time I go, I am afraid they will be gone like so many others. I hold my breath until I get to the driveway and see them, then breathe a sigh of relief.

A favorite barn of mine that is half gone now. Time always wins.

Above: Tenold Creamery when I first starting photographing it. The roof is caved in quite a bit now.

Below left: Tenold creamery, with the slate roof collapsing.

Below right: I think these old wooden silos were made of redwood, but I can't be sure. They are amazing works of art, inside and out.

Silver Lake creamery. It was a horse barn for many years. Now it sits empty.

Creamery in Hanlontown.

So many times, I have driven to a favorite place (actually, they are all favorites) only to find it gone. I drive up and down the road thinking maybe I missed it or am on the wrong road. Then I see evidence of what used to be a driveway. Now it is a field. The entire acreage, trees, barns, pump house, silo, windmill and house, completely disappeared. I feel such a loss. I feel it way down deep and it makes me want to cry. So many memories gone. So many treasures gone. I didn't even know the people who owned it and I grieve. I wonder if I am being overdramatic about it, but now that I know other people share this passion, I know I am not alone.

House put out to pasture near Britt. There were horses grazing around this beauty.

There are a couple of old one-room schoolhouses I have come across. Most of them are quite boarded up, but I learned the story of one of them. After this school closed, it was sold to a farmer who used it to store grain. The weight of the grain brought down the floor of the school. Then the back wall of the school came down, too. There was even the old wood heating stove left in the basement. It had been a beautiful building at one time.

Above: I think this used to be a schoolhouse. Many of these buildings were used as township meeting buildings when the schools moved out.

Below: The front door sports gorgeous trim and bits of the curtain that haven't disintegrated.

A schoolhouse in the woods. It was used for grain storage until the floor gave in.

The result of using a wood floor for grain storage.

One of the most fascinating discoveries I have made is the inside tops of the silos. I don't think I have seen two alike. While many tops are totally missing, the ones that are left are amazing works of art. There are brick, wood, and metal varieties. I do wish I could have been there to see how these were made. The bricks are so pretty and bright since the sun hasn't had a chance to fade them. The tin roofs appear like a star-filled sky when the light shines through the tiny holes. It is a bit tricky getting a good shot of them, but when the sky cooperates, they turn out well.

Above left: This was a unique silo top, because it was one of two silos built together with one roof that covered both.

Above right: This silo top appears to be either made of concrete or the bricks are totally covered by it. I don't think I have ever seen two alike.

Above left: Moss grows on the inside of the silo where the sun can't reach.

Above right: This aluminum silo roof looks like a starry night to me. You can find such soft beauty in odd places.

Below: A beautifully weathered home getting lost in the weeds.

I love getting shots of sun stars coming in through the holes of roofs. The barn in this shot stood for only a short time after I took this photo. It finally fell and the owner buried the remains. The other photo was a happy accident. Driving by this barn, we just happened to catch the sun shining through as it was setting.

Sunbeams in the dust make interesting shots, too. Even though having a hole in the roof is bad, it makes for some cool photos.

This is another one of my favorite shots. Catching the sun star through a hole in the roof is both sad and beautiful—sad because it means the roof is rotting away and beautiful because the sunlight shining through it so pretty. The barn has fallen down and is gone now.

Without the hole in the roof on the other side of the roof, this star would not be possible. But it still looks cool.

On our way home after a day of shooting, this scene caught my eye on a lonesome gravel road. I had to back up to get to just the right spot to catch the sun coming through both missing doors or windows at just the right time.

A sunbeam coming in through a hole in the roof of an old shed.

Almost every farmyard I encounter has a windmill or the remains of one. It is also common to see them standing alone out in a field or on a fence line. Vines use them as a trellis and swallow them. They are mistreated badly by people who use them for target practice. The ones that are still standing and twirling call out across the countryside with the most beautiful mournful songs. It sounds like they are trying so hard to make their voices heard and remembered. It is as if they know they won't be around much longer. Strong wind, rain, sleet, snow, and ice storms wreak havoc on them, as do flying branches. Sometimes they are so entangled in branches from nearby trees that they lose fan blades and other pieces and are no longer able to sing their sad songs.

Above: Windmill up on a hill.

Below left: What is left of a weathered windmill used for target practice.

Below right: The old windmill and house left with only each other for company.

I would call this a pumphouse, whether it is one or not. It was built close to the windmill. There were different placements for these houses. Some were built around the bottom of the windmill, others are off to the side, and some have none at all or they are long gone.

There is one house near Forest City that the vultures have claimed. They sit on the top of the house as if it is their own. They are very intimidating creatures but are much more afraid of us than we are of them. They are becoming more plentiful in our area. They roost on the tops of any old abandoned structure. You can see them from quite a distance away because of their size. They will only let you get so close before they take off. I haven't had the chance to see one of their nests yet, but I am always on the lookout for them. I figure if they are roosting on the roof of a house or barn, they might have a nest built inside or near.

Moss, mold, lichen, and who knows what else growing on this house near Forest City.

Vultures sit and watch as we park and get out of the car to get a closer look at their perch.

This house near Carpenter must have been such a beauty for most of the years of its life. The trim in the peaks is very lavish and the windows, even up in the attic, were leaded glass. It is such a shame to see it in the state it is in now. The inside is filled with old furniture and the weight of it all has collapsed the floor. The old cast iron heating radiators are still there and if you have ever tried to move one of those, you know they are mighty heavy. I threatened to bring a chainsaw with me the next time I came to visit this house so I could get better views of it. It sure makes one wonder how long this house has been sitting empty to have this much decay. I know of a house just a mile from me that has been sitting abandoned for almost forty years. Though it is losing the battle with time, it isn't in as bad of shape as this house, so I assume this one has been vacant fifty years or more.

This beautiful house near Carpenter truly is heartbreaking. It was so fancy when it was new. To see it in this shape is sad. It was full of junk furniture and ornate cast iron radiators.

When I visit these abandoned houses, I am careful to look for little items to tell me about the people who used to live here. This house, just east of Interstate 35 and a few miles south of the border, gave me a clue. I was leaning in through a window taking pictures when I looked down and something shiny caught my eye. I picked it up and it was a little cardboard box that was falling apart. The contents were shining through. Inside was a medal. It belonged to a soldier from World War I. I had a devil of a time reading who the person was, but it had Ransom County, ND, on it. We ended up going to a car show in Fort Ransom, ND, where there was an antique store that incidentally had a book with the names of the people from Ransom County who were in that war. There was a person's name in the book that matched what I could make out on the medal. It told where his last known relatives were. I called them and discovered they were indeed his relatives. I boxed this treasure up and sent it to them. I never did hear back to see if they got it but was happy knowing I tried. That is the one rare occasion where I was compelled to take something from a site. I normally wouldn't do anything like that, but I felt this medal needed to go somewhere. If I left it where it was, it would be lost forever.

This is one time when I did take something from a house. I could not leave the war medal I found just lay there. I found the family of the recipient and sent it to them.

This stove piece was in a pile of discarded cast-iron stove parts. I was able to buy it from the owner. I had to go back twice before I found the little missing piece under her chin.

There are so many fine details at work in this old house. It really is sad that no one loves her anymore.

Notice how the boards under the siding were cut and assembled at the diagonal. I never would have seen that if the siding had not been falling off. And check out those fancy doors!

The details on the outside of this house were a telltale sign that the people who built it really cared about how it looked.

Left: The soft filtered light coming in through the dirty windows makes for good black-and-white photos.

Below: Another shot of the incredible details on this massive house.

Barns take on different shapes when someone thinks they have a better idea. Like mousetraps! These first two barns are round, as you can see, and they have the silo up the middle. The stalls for the cattle were around the outer perimeter of the barn and the sileage would feed out the bottom of the silo so they could easily feed the critters. Being round may have been a wind resistant design. The one with no roof is past preservation, but the other is fixable. Unfortunately, the price to bring them back is far too high for most people, especially since they are no longer being used.

This was an odd little building. It was completely made of cement. It appeared to be a milk house so I assume the milk would stay colder longer. One might think it would be a smokehouse, but it wasn't all smoke-stained inside. It certainly has stood the test of time. As you can see, the date on it says 1910.

I think this must have been a milk house. The entire structure was made of concrete, including the roof.

What is left of a round barn near Forest City. In this one, you can see the silo still standing in the middle.

A round barn near Scarville. It's too costly to replace the roof.

It looks like this round roof barn lost the end first and just squatted down on its knees.

I am thinking this was once a house made into a barn with a rain shelter.

Crumbling foundation means this one may not last much longer. Not only that, but it is really tempting to draw a smile on this photo!

This must have been a huge farm operation at one time.

Falling fence in the fall.

My friend, Ray, let me take some friends on a barn tour with our cameras. This barn is beginning to falter now. And, Ray has passed away.

This barn always seemed so perfect to me but time and gravity won again and took it down.

Here is an old teeter-totter that someone's grandpa must have pieced together from old tractor parts. It was tangled in the raspberry brush. I imagine the children spending hours on it. He even made it adjustable for kids of all sizes.

This is a picture of a workshop that was long abandoned and is gone now. It was destroyed at the same time the barn was burned. They pushed it into the pile with the rubble that was buried. It was parts of a house from down the road a couple miles. It was disassembled and brought to this little clearing in the woods and put back together in a different configuration to make a workshop. It had a garage door on the east end so a car could be driven in to be worked on. The shop was in the west end with a workbench and a small wood stove to keep them warm. It also had an upper level. I miss this little shack as it made for some colorful photos and had many interesting things inside. It makes you wonder how many projects came and went through these doors.

A child's see-saw made from tractor seats, steel poles, and coil springs. Some grandpa made some grandkids really happy!

Grandpa's workshop. This was a house from up the road that was moved and put together differently than its original configuration.

Even old birdhouses can be abandoned.

I hope this book will inspire a few more people to appreciate the beauty I see out in the countryside, hidden up those lonely country roads. I have barely scratched the surface showing these to you. There are many more. I have only ventured out between thirty to forty miles from my home. I am sure there are plenty of rural treasures that I have missed, even in my area. I will continue to go out and discover more to share. Please keep your eyes open and try to see these old farmsteads as the gems they are. They are the remaining remnants of our shared Midwestern farming history. They helped to create and enabled our way of life.

FINAL NOTE

I do hope you enjoyed this journey and will take a minute to photograph the treasures in your area, so they are not totally forgotten when they are gone. But always remember to be respectful at all times. Do not enter where it says, "No Trespassing." Leave no trace that you were there and leave everything exactly as you found it. Take only pictures. Oh, and be extremely careful walking around the old fallen buildings as there are dangers in many steps. Nails, critters, holes, and rusting barbed wire just wait for a victim to come along and leave some blood on its barbs!

If you enjoyed this book, please have a look at the others I have out, *Abandoned Southern Minnesota* and *Rusting Relics of Minnesota*. Thank you!

ABOUT THE AUTHOR

JULIE BRONSON is a self-taught photographer who loves ambling up and down seldom traveled gravel roads looking for farm places begging to have their photo taken. She can spot an abandoned house from miles away. Her fascination with the architecture of the past never grows old. The beauty of broken-down, tired, old, faded wood shows through in the photos she takes. Her photography has been shown in art galleries and other venues in Albert Lea, Owatonna, Austin, and Faribault, Minnesota, and in Clear Lake, Iowa. She can always be found with a camera in hand, recording details of the past to preserve for the future.